E. B. Hopkins

The Gospel Trumpet

For the use of missionary societies and children's bands

E. B. Hopkins

The Gospel Trumpet
For the use of missionary societies and children's bands

ISBN/EAN: 9783337314637

Printed in Europe, USA, Canada, Australia, Japan

Cover: Foto ©Lupo / pixelio.de

More available books at **www.hansebooks.com**

THE

GOSPEL TRUMPET

FOR THE USE OF MISSIONARY SOCIETIES AND CHILDREN'S BANDS.

BY

MRS. E. B. HOPKINS,

BOSTON:
McDONALD, GILL & CO.,
36 BROMFIELD STREET.
1890.

Dedication.

PREFACE.

"And it shall come to pass in that day, that the great trumpet shall be blown, and they shall come which were ready to perish in the land of Assyria, and the outcasts in the land of Egypt, and shall worship the Lord in the holy mount at Jerusalem."—ISA. 27 : 13.

"Lift up thy voice like a trumpet."

THIS little collection is sent out with the earnest prayer that it may add to the interest and profit of societies and bands using it. I love these grand old missionary hymns, and have felt them to be an inspiration and help thus far in life; therefore I have selected many of them for this work, and ask the leaders not to pass them by, but teach them to the little ones. May the hearts of old and young, who may use any of these hymns, be stirred, and a love for missions and missionary work be increased.

MRS. E. B. HOPKINS.

MADISON, N.Y., December, 1889.

THE
GOSPEL TRUMPET.

1. ### The Year of Jubilee.
(LENOX. H. M.)

1. Blow ye the trum-pet, blow— The glad - ly sol - emn sound!
2. Ex - alt the Lamb of God, The sin a - ton - ing Lamb;
3. The Gos - pel trum-pet hear, The news of pard'ning grace;
4. Je - sus, our Great High Priest, Has full a - tone-ment made;

Let all the na - tions know, To earth's re - mot - est bound,
Re - demp-tion by His blood 'Thro' all the lands pro - claim,
Ye hap - py souls draw near, Be - hold your Sav - iour's face;
Ye wea - ry spir - its, rest, Ye mourn-ful souls, be glad;

The year of ju - bi - lee is come, The

The year of ju - bi - lee is come, The year of ju - bi -

year of ju - bi - lee is come; Re-turn ye ransom'd sin - ners, home.

lee is come; Re-turn, ye ran - - som'd sin - ners, home.

5

2. Gather the Reapers Home.

JENNIE JOHNSON.   JNO. R. SWENEY. By per.

1. Have ye heard the song from the golden land? Have ye heard the glad new song,
2. They are looking down from the golden land, Our beloved are look-ing down,
3. O the song rolls on from the golden land, And our hearts are strong to-day,
4. O the song rolls on from the golden land, From its vales of joy and flowers,

Let us bind our sheaves with a willing hand, For the time will not be long.
They have done their work, they have borne their cross, And received their promised
[crown.
For it nerves our souls with its mu-sic sweet, And we toil in the noon-tide ray.
And we feel and know by a liv-ing faith That its tones will soon be ours.

REFRAIN.

The Lord of the har-vest will soon ap-pear, His

smile, His voice we shall see and hear, The Lord of the har-vest will

soon ap-pear And gath-er the reap-ers home.

6

3. The Little Builders.

MARIA A. WEST.   Mrs. E. B. HOPKINS.

1. Lit - tle build-ers all are we, Build-ers for e - ter - ni - ty;
2. One by one the stones we lay, Build-ing slow - ly day by day;
3. Building in vast Chi - na, too, Liv - ing tem-ples rise to view;

Children of the Mission Bands, Working with our hearts and hands,
Building by our love are we, In the lands be-yond the sea;
Building in Ja-pan as well, Ah, what sto-ries we could tell!

Build-ing tem-ples for our King By the of - fer - ings we bring.
Build-ing by each tho't and prayer For the souls that suf - fer there;
And one day our eyes shall see, In a glad e - ter - ni - ty,

Liv - ing tem-ples He doth raise, Filled with life and light and praise.
Building in the Hin-doo land, Where the i - dols are as sand.
"Liv-ing stones" we helped to bring For the pal - ace of our King.

7

4.

The Lord's Vineyard.

"Go work to-day in my vineyard."—"The harvest truly is great, but the laborers are few."

WM. B. BRADBURY.

Spirited.

1. Go work to - day in the vine-yard of the Lord, Work, work to-day,
2. Go seek the lost who have wandered from the fold, Work, work to-day,
3. Glad news, glad news to the low - ly one proclaim, Work, work to-day,

work, work to-day; To those who toil He has promised a re-ward,
work, work to-day; In guilt and sin they perhaps are grow-ing old,
work, work to-day; Good will to man thro' a dy-ing Saviour's name,

Work, work to - day, work to - day; For a crown of life you may
Work, work to - day, work to - day; For a word may fall or a
Work, work to - day, work to - day; O, the time is short, it will

win and wear, In your Fa-ther's house there are man-sions fair.
tear may start, That will find its way to some grate - ful heart.
soon be o'er, And the night will come ye can work no more.

CHORUS.

Go work to-day, go work to-day, Go work in the vineyard of the Lord,

The Lord's Vineyard. Concluded.

Go work to-day, go work to-day, Go work in the vineyard of the Lord.

5. Who Will Gather in the Grain?

H. H. PENDLETON.

1. O! the fields are ripe with harvest, And the Mas - ter calls a - gain,
2. Now in youth's bright golden morning, Hear the Saviour's voice so plain,
3. O! if we would dwell in heav-en, With the ho - ly an - gel train.

If ye stand here i - dly wait-ing, Who will gath-er in the grain?
If ye love not one an - oth - er, Who will gath-er in the grain?
We must la - bor in the vine-yard Of the Master's ripened grain.

CHORUS.

We will work, yes, work for Je - sus, And He shall not call in vain,

Since the fields are ripe with har-vest, We will gath-er in the grain.

Used by per. of JAMES BAXTER, owner of Copyright.
9

6. **Little Travellers Zionward.**

1. Lit - tle travellers Zi - on-ward, Each one entering in - to rest,
2. Who are they whose lit - tle feet, Pac - ing life's dark journey through,
3. All their earth-ly jour-ney past, Ev - ery tear and pain gone by,

In the king-dom of our Lord, In the man-sions of the blest,
Now have reached that heav'nly seat They have ev - er kept in view?
Here to - geth-er met at last, At the por-tal of the sky!

There to wel-come Je - sus waits, Gives the crown His followers win,
"I, from Greenland's fro-zen land;" "I, from In - dia's sul-try plain;"
Each the wel-come "Come" awaits, Conqueror o - ver death and sin:

Lift your heads, ye gold-en gates, Let the lit - tle traveller in.
"I, from Af-ric's bar-ren sand:" "I, from isl-ands of the main.
Lift your heads, ye gold-en gates, Let the lit - tle travellers in.

7. The Kingdom is Coming.

Words Adapted by G. E. L.   Jno. R. Sweney. By per.

1. In all the bright fac - es of earth's heav'nly plac - es, Be-
2. From the bright crys-tal fount-ains Of God's ho - ly mountains, O
3. With the Lamb on the throne, in the midst of His own, By the

hold how the Spir - it doth shine, Our Lord doth pos - sess them, His
see how the pure wa-ters flow. The des - erts are blooming, The
banks of Life's riv - er we'll stand. Re-deemed from de-struc-tion, To

pres-ence doth bless them, They're filled with the Spir - it di - vine.
earth they're per-fum - ing, The na - tions their Sav-iour do know.
sing res - ur - rec - tion, A sin-conqu'ring, glo - ri - fied band.

D.S. knowl-edge and glo - ry, As wa - ters that cov - er the sea.

Chorus.

The Kingdom is com-ing, Go tell ye the sto - ry, God's

ban - ner ex - alt - ed we see. The earth He doth fill With His

11

8. Cast Thy Bread Upon the Waters.

1. Cast thy bread up - on the wa - ters, Ye who have but scant sup-ply,
2. Cast thy bread up - on the wa - ters, Poor and wea-ry, worn with care,—
3. Cast thy bread up - on the wa - ters, Ye who have a - bun-dant store;
4. Cast thy bread up - on the wa - ters, Far and wide your treasures strew,
5. Cast thy bread up - on the wa - ters, Waft it on with pray-ing breath,

An - gel eyes will watch a - bove it;— You shall find it by and by!
Oft - en sit-ting in the shadow, Have you not a crumb to spare?
It may float on many a bil - low, It may strand on many a shore;
Scat-ter it with will-ing fin - gers, Shout for joy to see it go!
In some dis-tant, doubtful mo-ment, It may save a soul from death;

He who in his righteous bal-ance Doth each hu - man ac - tion weigh
Can you not to those a-round you Sing some lit - tle song of hope,
You may think it lost for-ev - er, But, as sure as God is true,
For if you do close-ly keep it, It will on - ly drag you down;
When you sleep in sol-emn si - lence, 'Neath the morn and evening dew,

Will your sac - ri - fice re-mem-ber, Will your lov-ing deeds re-pay?
As you look with longing vis - ion Thro' faith's mighty tel - e - scope?
In this life or in the oth - er, It will yet re - turn to you.
If you love it more than Je - sus, It will keep you from your crown.
Stranger hands, which you have strengthened, May strew lil-ies o - ver you.

Used by per. JOHN J. HOOD owner of Copyright

9. After the Harvest, Golden Sheaves.

Mrs. MARY E. KAIL.   J. R. MURRAY.

1. Af-ter the harvest, golden sheaves; And when, the har-ves-ter's work is done,
2. Af-ter the harvest, golden sheaves; Gathered a-round at the Master's feet,
3. Af-ter the harvest, golden sheaves; Ye, who are sow-ing your seed in tears,
4. Af-ter the harvest, golden sheaves; Tho' the toil-ers for heav-en be few,
5. Af-ter the harvest, golden sheaves; Then let us work while the days are long,

Joy, and glo-ry, and perfect peace,— In the new life, be-gun.
'Mid sweet songs of tri-umph-ant praise, Mak-ing our joy com-plete.
For the fruit of the work you do, Waiting for ma-ny years.
Hands that are will-ing can always find Plen-ty of work, to do.
When the Lord of the harvest comes, Join in the reap-er's song.

REFRAIN.

This shall the song of the reap-er be, Rest, at closing of day for me;

Then, on the bless-ed Redeemer's breast, I shall lie down to blissful rest.

13

10. The Calling of the Children.

"Come over into Macedonia, and help us."—Acts 16: 9.

Rev. J. E. RANKIN, D. D.   Old German Air.

1. Hear ye not the children call-ing From the land be - yond the sea,
2. Shall we let these children per-ish, Nor to them the gos-pel give?
3. Tho' you can-not cross the o - cean, You can build the ships that sail;

Shrouded in a night ap - pall-ing, Vic-tims of i - dol - a - try?
Shall we hide the Lord we cher-ish, While they, too, might look and live?
You can show your high de - vo-tion By your gifts which nev-er fail;

Like the o - cean, sad - ly moaning, Come, they say, and give us light;
Send the tid-ings on wind's pinions, Till they reach earth's farthest bounds;
You can of - fer, night and morning, Prayer to God who gave His Son,

Tell us of the Lamb a - ton-ing, Ere we sink in end-less night.
Pub - lish it in sin's do - min-ion, What a Sav-iour you have found.
That on them the true light dawning, To our Lord they may be won.

Per. of J. W. BISCHOFF.

14

11. Entire Consecration.

FRANCES RIDLEY HAVERGAL. Chorus by W. J. K. WM. J. KIRKPATRICK.

1. Take my life, and let it be Con-se-crat-ed, Lord, to Thee;
2. Take my feet, and let them be Swift and beau-ti-ful for Thee;
3. Take my lips, and let them be Filled with mes-sag-es for Thee;
4. Take my moments and my days, Let them flow in end-less praise;

Take my hands and let them move At the im-pulse of Thy love.
Take my voice and let me sing Al-ways, on-ly for my King.
Take my sil-ver and my gold,— Not a mite would I with-hold.
Take my in-tel-lect, and use Ev-ery power as Thou shalt choose.

CHORUS.

{ Wash me in the Saviour's precious blood, the precious blood,
{ Cleanse me in its pu-ri-fy-ing flood, the heal-ing flood, } Lord, I give to

Thee, my life and all, to be, Thine, henceforth, e-ter-nal-ly.

5 Take my will, and make it Thine;
It shall be no longer mine;
Take my heart,—it is Thine own,—
It shall be Thy royal throne.

6 Take my love,—my Lord, I pour
At Thy feet its treasure-store!
Take myself, and I will be
Ever, only, all for Thee!

By permission.

15

12. The Children's Army.

GEO. COOPER. Air—"Glory Hallelujah."

1. There's a grand and no-ble ar - my that is gath-'ring for the fight, And it
2. In the field and on the ocean, where there's manly work to do,— In the
3. They are marching, and their banners wave upon the ra-diant air; Oh, the

soon will strike the victor's blow with cour-age and with might; Oh, it
high and no-ble pla - ces where the la - bor - ers are few, Oh, the
world is all be-fore them, and the way is bright and fair, For they

marches on, with faces ev-er beaming with delight, To conquer ev - er-more.
Future will behold them, for their hearts are bold and true, To conquer ev - er-more.
gather in life's morning, firm resolved to do and dare, And conquer ev - er-more.

CHORUS.

Hail, the ar - my of the chil-dren, Hail, the ar-my of the children!

Hail, the ar-my of the chil-dren, Hip, hip, hip, hip, hur-rah!

16

13.   Freely Speak for Jesus.

Mrs. E. C. ELLSWORTH.   T. C. O'KANE.

1. Oh, free - ly speak for Je - sus,— Pro - claim how great His love;
2. Go, bear a - mid the dark-ness Some beams of gos-pel light,
3. Oh, gent - ly lift the fal - len; Let love her man-tle spread;
4. The small - est act for Je - sus Shall glow with grace di - vine,

Oh, tell that sweet com-pas - sion Once brought Him from a - bove.
'Till hope shall clear each path-way Now shroud-ed dark as night.
Then bear the lost to Je - sus, Who once for sin-ners bled.
And peace that pass-eth knowedge Shall ev - er-more be thine.

CHORUS.

Yes, fill thy life with ser-vice, Oh, fill it to the brim; -

Christ wrought for thee a blessing: Then do thy best for Him.

14. Christ's Little Soldiers.

JULIA A. MATHEWS.   J. R. M.

1. We are sol-diers of the Lord, 'Neath His flag we're called to fight;
2. Strong and sub-tle is our foe, But our Lord is strong-er still;
3. Though we fal-ter on the road, He will nev-er chide nor frown,
4. All He asks is loy-al love, Earnest ef-fort for the right;

Sin and e-vil are our foes, We are bat-tling for the right.
He will guide us as we go, He'll de-fend us from all ill.
For He knew how weak we were When He chose us for His own.
For the bat-tle is His own, We shall win it by His might.

REFRAIN.

Come and join our lit-tle band, Come and join our lit-tle band,

We are sure to win the day, We have naught to dread or fear,

We have naught to dread or fear, For our Saviour, blessed Saviour leads the way.

15. What Shall I Do For Jesus.

THEO. F. SEWARD.

1. What shall I do for that kind Friend Who once for me so poor be-came;
2. For Him who bore my sins a-way, Who freely shed His blood for me,
3. For Him who, with such ten-der love, Bestows the rich-es of His grace;
4. I'll give to Him my heart and life, And love and serve Him day by day;

Who had not where to lay His head, Who suffered death, reproach, and shame.
Who sought me when I went a-stray, Redeemed my soul and made it free.
For Him who in-ter-cedes a-bove, And for my soul pre-pares a place.
And this shall be my on-ly strife, That from His fold I may not stray.

CHORUS.

What shall I do, What shall I do, What shall I do for Je-sus,
What shall I do, What shall I do, do, etc.
What can I do, What can I do, do, etc.
This can I do, This can I do, do, etc.

What shall I do, What shall I do for that kind friend.

16. Lights for All.

ANNA WARNER. Mrs. E. B. HOPKINS.

1. Je - sus bids us shine With a pure, clear light, Like a lit - tle can - dle
2. Je - sus bids us shine First of all for Him; Well He sees and knows it
3. Je - sus bids us shine, Yes, for all a - round; O! what depths of darkness

Burn-ing in the night, For the world is dark - ness, So
If our light be dim. He looks down from heav - en To
In the world are found! There's sin, there's want and sor - row, So

we must shine, You in your small cor - ner And I in mine.
see us shine, You in your small cor - ner And I in mine.
we must shine, You in your small cor - ner And I in mine.

Lord, Dismiss Us.

WALTER SHIRLEY. THOMAS HASTINGS.

1. { Lord, dismiss us with thy blessing, Fill our hearts with joy and peace ; }
   { Let us each, thy love possessing, Triumph in redeeming grace : } O re-

fresh us, Traveling thro' this wilderness. O refresh us, Traveling thro' this wilderness.

2 Thanks we give, and adoration,
  For thy Gospel's joyful sound ;
May the fruits of thy salvation
  In our hearts and lives abound ;
    May thy presence
  With us evermore be found.

3 So, whene'er the signal's given,
  Us from earth to call away,
Borne on angels' wings to heaven,
  Glad the summons to obey,
    May we ever
  Reign with Christ in endless day.

17. Beautiful Child of the Manger.

Words and Music by N. S. HOWARD.

1. When the beautiful light from the heavens Shone over the plains a - far,
2. Of the birth of the infant Redeemer, The wondrous atonement for sin,
3. Of the glo-ri-ous plan of redemption, God gave to the world here below,
4. Then.. sing ye a-loud his high praises, Let mel - o - dy fill the air;

The angels were bearing glad tidings Of Bethlehem's wonderful Star.
Whose cra-dle was on-ly a manger In the sta - ble of an inn.
That all who believe on the Saviour The joys of salvation might know.
For with Jesus, our blessed Redeemer, The glo - ries of heav'n we'll share.

CHORUS.

O, beau-ti-ful child of the manger, O Je - sus, our Saviour and King;

With hearts fill'd with joy and with gladness, Our tributes of praise we bring.

18. Marching Onward.

Mrs. R. N. Turner.   Wm. J. Kirkpatrick.

1. We are marching, marching onward, Strong to dare, and strong to do!
2. As He leads us, so we'll fol - low, For His light il - lumes our way;
3. We are marching, marching onward With a cour - age true and strong;

With our ban - ner float-ing o'er us, And our Lead-er, Christ in view!
Ev - er on-ward, ev - er on-ward, Step by step, and day by day!
For the vic-t'ry shall not fail us, Tho' the war-fare may be long!

Sin, with all its tempting pleasures, Beckons us with lur - ing hand;
'Tis a grand and glo-rious ar-my; And the King whose name we bear,
No! the heart that trusts in Je - sus Shall not fall in weak-ness down;

But with true and earnest pur-pose, For our Mas-ter we will stand.
Watches o'er us, and sus-tains us, With a strong and ten-der care!
Strength He gives, the cross to car-ry, Strength to win the vic-tor's crown!

CHORUS.

March-ing on - ward, marching on - ward. Bear-ing forth the
Marching onward, marching on - ward,

22

Marching Onward. <small>Concluded.</small>

ban-ner of the pure and free; Marching on - ward, march-ing
March-ing on - ward,

on - ward; Christ our Lead-er prom-is - es the vic - to - ry.
Marching on-ward;

19.   The Song of Jubilee.   7s.

LEONARD BACON.

1. Wake the song of Ju - bi - lee,   Let it ech - o o'er the sea.
2. All ye na-tions, join and sing,   Christ, of lords and kings, is King;
3. Now the des-ert lands re - joice,   And the isl - ands join their voice—

Now is come the promised hour;   Je - sus reigns with sov'reign power.
Let it sound from shore to shore,   Je - sus reigns for - ev - er - more.
Yea, the whole cre - a - tion sings,   Je - sus is the King of Kings.

Wake the song of Ju - bi - lee,   Let it e - cho o'er the sea.
Wake the song of Ju - bi - lee,   Let it e - cho o'er the sea.
Wake the song of Ju - bi - lee,   Let it e - cho o'er the sea.

23

20. Help Just a Little.

Music from "The Wells of Salvation,"
new words by Rev. W. A. SPENCER.

WM. J. KIRKPATRICK.

1. Broth-er for Christ's kingdom sighing, Help a lit-tle, help a lit-tle;
2. Is thy cup made sad by tri - al? Help a lit-tle, help a lit-tle;
3. Tho' no wealth to thee is giv-en, Help a lit-tle, help a lit-tle;

Help to save the mil-lions dy-ing, Help just a lit-tle.
Sweet-en it with self-de-ni-al, Help just a lit-tle.
Sac-ri-fice is gold in heav-en, Help just a lit-tle.

CHORUS.

Oh, the wrongs that we may righten! Oh, the hearts that we may lighten!

Oh, the skies that we may brighten! Helping just a lit-tle.

4 Let us live for one another,
  Help a little, help a little;
  Help to lift each fallen brother,
  Help just a little.

5 Tho' thy life is pressed with sorrow,
  Help a little, help a little;
  Bravely look t'ward God's to-morrow,
  Help just a little.

21. Work for the Master.

"The harvest truly is plenteous, but the laborers are few." —Matt. 9: 37.

FANNIE J. KENNISH.   T. MARTIN TOWNE.

1. Lo! the sum-mer sun is shin-ing On the fields of rip-en'd grain,
2. Do not hope for rich-er harvests, Do not wait for whit-er fields;
3. Tho' an - oth - er wield the sick-le, Your re-ward may yet be won;

And the har-vest-ers are tell-ing Of the toil for hand and brain;
Do the task that God assigned you, Trust in Him for great - er yields;
You may glean be - hind the reap-er, Waiting for the glad "Well done;"

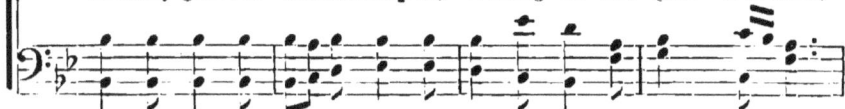

On the hill-side, in the val-ley, Shining blades are flash-ing thro';
There are man-y fields of la - bor Needing workmen brave and true;
If you're working for the Mas-ter, You will find e-nough to do;

For the har-vest now is near-ing, And the la - bor - ers are few.
For the har-vest is a-bund-ant, And the la - bor - ers are few.
For the har-vest is a-bund-ant, And the la - bor - ers are few.

Per. of J. W. BISCHOFF.

22. Glory, Hallelujah!

Words by Miss ABBY SHAW.

1. We have gird-ed on our ar-mor in a Christian war-fare here, Our
2. With such a lead-er who can doubt, the strug-gle e'er give o'er, Un-
3. God grant where er-ror now prevails, truth soon may reign instead, Thro'
4. Then as each sol-dier of the cross the fi-nal vict-'ry won, Shall

Cap-tain is the same to-day, with-out reproach or fear, As
til the standard of the cross shall float from shore to shore, Till
clouds of su-per-sti-tion dark now frown-ing o-ver-head, The
stand be-fore the throne of God and His be-lov-ed Son, What

when in Israel's camp he stood, a fie-ry pil-lar near, Our God will lead us on.
ev'ry tongue confess our Lord, and praise Him evermore. Our God will lead us on.
Sun of Righteousness His beam on ev'ry land shall shed. Our God will lead us on.
joy for us if He shall say, Faithful and good, well done. Our God will lead us on.

CHORUS.

Glo-ry, glo-ry, hal-le-lu-jah! Glo-ry, glo-ry, hal-le-lu-jah!

Glo-ry, glo-ry, hal-le-lu-jah! Our God will lead us on.

26

23. Watchman, Tell Me. 8s & 7s. Double.

Moderato.

1. Watchman, tell me, does the morning Of fair Zi - on's glo - ry dawn?
2. Watchman, see, the light is beam - ing, Brighter still up - on the way;
3. Watchman, hail, the light as-cend-ing, Of the grand Sab-bat - ic year;

Have the signs that mark its com - ing Yet up - on its path-way shone?
Signs thro' all the earth are gleaming, O-mens of the com-ing day
All with voic - es loud pro-claim-ing That the kingdom's ve - ry near:

Pil-grim, yes! a - rise, look round thee; Light is breaking in the skies;
When the Ju-bal trum-pet sounding, Shall awake from earth and sea,
Pil-grim, yes, I see just yon-der, Canaan's glorious heights a - rise,

Gird thy bri - dal robes a-round thee, Morn-ing dawns, a - rise, a - rise!
And the saints of God now sleeping, Clad in im - mor-tal - i - ty.
Sa - lem too ap-pears in grandeur, Towering 'neath its sun-lit skies.

4 Watchman, in the golden city,
  Seated on His jasper throne,
Zion's king enthroned in beauty,
  Reigns in peace from zone to zone;
There on sun-lit hills and mountains,
  Golden beams serenely glow;
Purling streams and crystal fountains,
  On whose banks sweet flow'rets blow.

5 Watchman, see, the land is nearing,
  With its vernal fruits and flowers,
On just yonder, O how cheering
  Bloom forever Eden's bowers!
Hark! the choral strains are ringing,
  Wafted on the balmy air,
See the millions, hear them singing,
  Soon the pilgrim will be there.

27

24. Lo, the Golden Fields are Smiling.

FANNY J. CROSBY. WM. J. KIRKPATRICK. By per.

1. Lo, the gold-en fields are smil-ing, Wherefore i - dle shouldst thou be?
2. Take the balm of con - so - la - tion That so oft has cheered thy heart;
3. Go and gath-er souls for Je - sus, Pre-cious souls thy love may win;
4. Go then, work, the Mas - ter call-eth, Go, no lon - ger i - dle be;

Great the har-vest, few the work-ers, And the Lord hath need of thee.
Let some wea - ry broth-er toil - er In thy com-fort share a part.
Lead them to the door of mer - cy, Tell them how to en - ter in,
Waste no more thy precious mo-ments, For the Lord hath need of thee.

Go and work, the time is wan - ing, Let thy earnest heart re - ply
Go and lift the heav-y bur - den He has struggled long to bear,
Go and gath-er souls for Je - sus, Work while strength and breath remain.
Once He gave His life thy ran - som, That thy soul with Him might live,

ad lib.

To the call so oft re - peat - ed, "Blessed Mas-ter, here am I."
Go and kneeling down be-side him, Blend thy faith with his in prayer.
What are years of con-stant la - bor, To the joy thou yet shall gain.
Now the ser-vice He de-mand-eth, Can thy heart re - fuse to give?

REFRAIN.

Hark, the song, the song of bus - y work-ers, In the fields so fair to see;

Lo, the Golden Fields. Concluded.

ad lib.

Go and fill thy place a-mong them, For the Lord hath need of thee.

25. Over the Ocean Wave.

WILLIAM B. BRADBURY.

1. O - ver the o - cean wave, far, far a - way, There the poor
2. Here in this hap - py land we have the light Shin - ing from
3. Then, while the mis-sion ships glad tid - ings bring, List! as that

CHORUS.—Pit - y them, pit - y them, Christians at home, Haste with the

FINE.

heath - en live, wait - ing for day; Grop - ing in ig - no-rance,
God's own word, free, pure, and bright; Shall we not send to them
heath - en band joy - ful - ly sing, "O - ver the o - cean wave,

bread of life, has - ten and come.

D.C. Chorus.

dark as the night, No bless-ed Bi - ble to give them the light.
Bi - bles to read, Teachers, and preachers, and all that they need?
O, see them come, Bringing the bread of life, guid-ing us home."

26. Young Soldiers of the Cross.

Mrs. E. M. SANGSTER.

f Spirited and Energetic.

1. The sa-cred ban-ner of the Cross, The pledge of vic-tory won
2. On Jor-dan's bank, on Olives' mount, And all those dew-y plains
3. Je-ru-sa-lem shall yet re-joice To hail Mes-si-ah's reign;

By Him who in His anguish cried, "Thy will, not mine be done."
Where Ju-dah's harp in hap-pier times Rang out its tune-ful strains;
The sol-i-ta-ry place be glad, The des-ert bloom a-gain;

Ye, who have borne thro' many a field Its blood-stain'd col-ors fair,
Its chords are mute—their song no more A-wakes the trembling air;
Her ru-in'd towers, her crumbled walls, Their an-cient glo-ry wear;

Go where your dear Re-deem-er trod, And plant that standard there.
Yet Je-sus trod those love-ly wilds: Go plant that standard there.
The crescent to the Cross shall bend, Go plant that standard there.

FULL CHORUS.

f

A beau-ti-ful crown is waiting for you, Far a-way in the promis'd land;

Composed for, and sung at.
the 48th Anniversary of the New York Sunday School Union, May 10th, 1864.

Young Soldiers of the Cross. Concluded.

A beau-ti-ful crown is waiting for me, Far a-way in the promis'd land.

27. O What Can Little Hands Do?

J. R. M.

1. O what can lit-tle hands do, To please the King of Heaven?
2. O what can lit-tle lips do, To please the King of Heaven?
3. O what can lit-tle eyes do, To please the King of Heaven?
4. O what can lit-tle hearts do, To please the King of Heaven?

The lit-tle hands some work may try That will some simple want sup-ply,
The lit-tle lips can praise and pray, And gen-tle words of kindness say,
The lit-tle eyes can up-ward look, Can learn to read God's Ho-ly book,
Young hearts, if He His Spir-it send, Can love Him, Maker, Saviour, Friend,

Such grace to mine be giv-en, Such grace to mine be given.
Such grace to mine be giv-en, Such grace to mine be given.
Such grace to mine be giv-en, Such grace to mine be given.
Such grace to mine be giv-en, Such grace to mine be given.

28. The Little Missionary.

Selected.

Mrs. E. B. Hopkins.

1. I may not go to In - dia, To Chi - na, or Ja - pan;
2. The lit-tle water-drops come down To make the flow - ers grow;
3. I'll be a mis-sion-ary now, And work the best I may;

To work for Je - sus here at home I'll do the best I can.
The lit - tle riv - u - lets flow on To bless where'er they go;
For if I want to work for God, There surely is a way.

I'll tell of His great love for me, And how I love *Him*, too;
The lit - tle seeds make mighty trees To cool us with their shade:
I'll pray for those who cross the sea, My offering, too, I'll send,

And, bet-ter far, I'll show my love In all that I may do.
If lit - tle things like these do good, To try I'm not a - fraid.
And do all that is in my power, This great bad world to mend.

1. From Greenland's i - cy moun-tains, From In - dia's cor - al strand,
2. What tho' the spi - cy breez - es Blow soft o'er Ceylon's isle;
3. Shall we, whose souls are light - ed With wis-dom from on high,
4. Waft, waft, ye winds, His sto - ry, And you, ye wa-ters, roll.

Where Af-ric's sun - ny foun - tains Roll down their gol-den sands;
Though ev - ery prospect pleas - es, And on - ly man is vile:
Shall we to men be - night - ed The lamp of life de - ny?
Till, like a sea of glo - ry, It spreads from pole to pole:

From ma-ny an-cient riv - er, From many a palmy plain,
In vain with lav - ish kind - ness The gifts of God are strown;
Sal - va - tion!—O sal - va - tion! The joy - ful sound pro - claim,
Till, o'er our ran-som'd na - ture The Lamb for sin-ners slain,

They call us to de - liv - er Their land from er-ror's chain.
The heath-en in his blind - ness Bows down to wood and stone.
Till earth's re - mot-est na - tion Has learn'd Mes-si-ah's name.
Re-deem - er, King, Cre - a - tor, In bliss re-turns to reign.

30. Lord, What Wilt Thou Have Me To Do?

CLAYES.

WM. J. KIRKPATRICK. By per.

1. Are you willing, my sister, my broth-er,   To work in the field of the   Lord?
2. Say   not, I   am humble and low-ly,   And lit-tle can do if I   would;
3. Do you pray to the "Lord of the harvest," That He would more laborers send

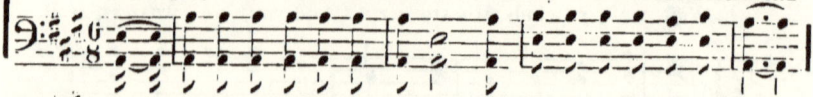

Would you gladly choose more than another, His service to gain His re - ward?
Re - mem - ber that Je-sus the Ho-ly, Said of one, "She hath done what she could."
To fields that from you are the farthest, Neglecting those you should have gleaned?

Seek not for a prom-i-nent sta - tion,   You zeal or your talent to   show;
Some names shall like stars shine for-ev-er, Which few of this world ever knew;
Cease not in the earnest pe - ti - tion, For   the lab'rers truly are   few,

But ask in some humble re - la-tion, "Lord, what wilt Thou have me to do?"
They sought with most earnest endeavor, "Lord, what wilt Thou have me to do?"
Rememb'ring to make this addition, "Lord, what wilt Thou have me to do?"

REFRAIN.

What wilt Thou have me to do, Lord? What wilt Thou have me to do?

Lord, What Wilt Thou. Concluded.

I ask seeking guidance from heaven, Lord, what wilt Thou have me to do?

31. The Battle Hymn of Missions.

RAY PALMER.   JOHN WHITAKER.

1. E - ter - nal Fa - ther, Thou hast said, That Christ all
2. We wait Thy tri - umph, Sav - iour King; Long a - ges
3. Thy hosts are mus - tered to the field; "The Cross! the
4. On moun - tain tops the watch - fires glow, Where scat - tered

glo - ry shall ob - tain; That He who once a
have pre - pared Thy way; Now all a - broad Thy
Cross!"the bat - tle call; The old grim tow'rs of
wide the watch - men stand; Voice ech - oes voice, and

suffer - er bled Shall o'er the world a con - qu'ror reign.
ban - ner fling, Set time's great bat - tle in ar - ray.
dark - ness yield, And soon shall tot - ter to their fall.
on - ward flow The joy - ous shouts from land to land.

5 O fill Thy Church with faith and power,
  Bid her long night of weeping cease ;
  To groaning nations haste the hour
  Of life and freedom, light and peace.

6 Come, Spirit, make Thy wonders known,
  Fulfill the Father's high decree ;
  Then earth, the might of hell o'erthrown,
  Shall keep her last great jubilee.

35

32. Something to Do in Heaven.

Words by R. S. TAYLOR.   WM. B. BRADBURY.

1. There'll be something in heav-en for chil-dren to do, None are
2. There'll be les-sons to learn of the wis-dom of God, As they
3. There'll be er-rands of love from the man-sions a-bove, To the

i-dle in that bless-ed land. There'll be loves for the heart, there'll be
wan-der the green meadows o'er; And they'll have for their teachers in
dear ones that lin-ger be-low; And it may be our Fa-ther the

thoughts for the mind, And em-ploy-ment for each lit-tle hand.
that blest a-bode, All the good that have gone there be-fore.
chil-dren will send, To be an-gels of mer-cy in woe.

FULL CHORUS.

There'll be something to do ; There'll be some-thing to do ; There'll be

something for chil-dren to do. On the bright shining shore, where there's

Used by per. of S. BRAINARD'S SONS, owners of Copyright.

36

Something to Do in Heaven. Concluded.

joy ev - er-more, There'll be some-thing for chil - dren to do.

33. Marching Hymn.

"But unto you that fear my name, shall the Sun of righteousness arise with. healing in his wings"—Mal. 4: 2.

BETH DAY.　　　　　　　　　　　　　　J. W. BISCHOFF. By per.

1. Like a band of sol - diers, As we march we sing,
2. For our lov - ing Sav - iour Work-ing all our days,

Un - ion is our watch - word, Loud our prais - es ring.
And for ev - ery vic - tory Giv - ing Him the praise.

Je - sus is our Cap - tain, We'll not work in vain,
Je - sus, our dear Sav - iour, Ev - er may we be

But to swell our ar - my Mem - bers try to gain.
Firm, de - cid - ed sol - diers, Serv - ing on - ly Thee.

34. Willing Workers.

"Juvenile Miss. Mag."

Jno. R. Sweney.

1. On - ly a band of chil - dren, sit - ting at Je - sus' feet,
2. Take us, dear Sav - iour, take us in - to Thy heavenly fold!
3. On - ly a band of chil - dren, sit - ting at Je - sus' feet,
4. Oh, with pure hearts and low - ly, help us, dear Lord, to go,

Fit - ing ourselves to en - ter in - to His ser - vice sweet,
Keep our feet from stray - ing out in the dark and cold.
Fit - ing ourselves to en - ter in - to His ser - vice sweet;
Bearing the glad, sweet sto - ry un - to sad hearts be - low;

Soft - ly His voice is call - ing, "Lit - tle one, come un - to Me!
Call us Thy "Lit - tle Help - ers," glad in Thy work to share;
Seeking His light to guide us wher - ev - er the way is dim;
And reaching the pearly por - tals, may the welcome sweet be given,—

Stay not, tho' weak and help - less. Child, I have need of *thee!*"
Make us Thine own dear chil - dren, wor - thy Thy name to bear.
Learn - ing His beau - ti - ful les - sons, long - ing to be like Him.
"Pass thro' the gate, My chil - dren, of such is the kingdom of heaven."

38

Willing Workers. Concluded.

CHORUS.

On - ly a band of chil - dren, sit - ting at Je - sus' feet,

Fit-ting our-selves to en - ter in - to His ser - vice sweet.

35. Mendon. L. M.

With Ardor.

1. Be-hold, the heathen waits to know The joy the Gos - pel will bestow;
2. Come, let us, with a grateful heart, In this blest la - bor share a part;
3. Our hearts exult in songs of praise, That we have seen these lat - ter days,
4. Where'er His hand hath spread the skies, Sweet incense to His Name shall rise;

The ex - iled cap-tive to re-ceive The freedom Je - sus has to give.
Our prayers and off'rings gladly bring To aid the tri-umphs of our King.
When our Re-deem-er shall be known, Where Sa-tan long hath held His throne.
And slave and freeman, Greek and Jew, By sov'reign grace be form'd a-new.

39

36. The Song of Triumph.

SALLIE SMITH.   JNO. R. SWENEY. By per.

1. We've list-ed in the roy-al ranks,and gird-ed on the sword,
2. We've list-ed in the roy-al ranks of our Re-deem-er King,
3. Yes, we shall con-quer thro' His grace,and gain the promised land,

And gird-ed on the sword, and gird-ed on the sword;
Of our Re-deem-er King, of our Re-deem-er King,
And gain the prom-ised land, and gain the prom-ised land,

And forth we march in ar-mor bright,our ban-ners wide un-furled,
And though the strife may fierce-ly rage, His praise we'll glad-ly sing,
Ar-rayed in robes of righteousness, with palms in ev-'ry hand;

Led on by Him who conquered death,and tri-umph o'er the world.
Who, out of all His faith-ful ones will more than conquerors bring.
Yes, we shall con-quer thro' His grace,and in His kingdom stand.

REFRAIN.

Re-joice, re-joice, re-joice, re-joice. His mighty shield is o'er us.

The Song of Triumph. Concluded.

He tells us not to fear, He tells us not to fear;

Re-joice, re-joice, re-joice, re-joice, The foe shall fall be-fore us!

A glo-rious time is com-ing soon, our vic-to-ry is near.

37. How To Do It.

Selected.   Mrs. E. B. Hopkins.

1. The fields are all white, And the reap-ers are few; We chil-dren are
2. Our hands are so small, And our words are so weak, We can-not teach
3. We'll work by our prayers, By the pen-nies we bring, By small self-de-
4. Un-til by and by, As the years pass at length, We too may be

will-ing, But what can we do To work for our Lord in His har-vest?
oth-ers; How then shall we seek To work for our Lord in His har-vest?
ni-als—The least lit-tle thing May work for our Lord in His har-vest.
reapers, And go forth in His strength To work for our Lord in His har-vest.

41

38. O Day of Rest and Gladness.

C. WORDSWORTH.

TUNE—"Mendebras. 7s, 6s."

1. O day of rest and glad-ness, O day of joy and light,
2. On thee, at the cre-a-tion, The light first had its birth;
3. To-day on wea-ry na-tions The heavenly man-na falls;
4. New gra-ces ev-er gain-ing From this our day of rest,

O balm of care and glad-ness, Most beau-ti-ful, most bright:
On thee, for our sal-va-tion, Christ rose from depths of earth;
To ho-ly con-vo-ca-tions The sil-ver trum-pet calls,
We reach the rest re-main-ing To spir-its of the blest;

On thee, the high and low-ly, Through a-ges joined in tune,
On thee, our Lord, vic-to-rious, The Spir-it sent from heaven;
Where gos-pel light is glow-ing With pure and ra-diant beams,
To Ho-ly Ghost be prais-es, To Fa-ther, and to Son;

Sing "Ho-ly, ho-ly, ho-ly," To the great God Tri-une.
And thus on thee, most glo-rious, A tri-ple light was given.
And liv-ing wa-ters flow-ing With soul-re-fresh-ing streams.
The Church her voice up-rais-es To thee, blest Three in One.

42

39. He Leadeth Me.

"The Lord is my Shepherd, I shall not want. He maketh me to lie down in green pastures;
He leadeth me beside the still waters."

WILLIAM B. BRADBURY.

1. He lead-eth me! O, blessed thought, O, words with ho-ly comfort fraught,
2. Sometimes 'mid scenes of deepest gloom, Sometimes where Eden's bowers bloom,
3. Lord, I would grasp Thy hand in mine, Nor ev-er mur-mur nor re-pine.
4. And when my task on earth is done, When, by Thy grace, the victory's won.

Whate'er I do, where'er I be, Still 'tis God's hand that leadeth me.
By wa-ters still, o'er troubled sea—Still 'tis His hand that leadeth me.
Con-tent, what-ev-er lot I see, Since 'tis my God that leadeth me.
E'en death's cold wave I will not flee, Since God thro' Jor-dan leadeth me.

REFRAIN.

He lead-eth me! He lead-eth me! By His own hand He lead-eth me;

His faith-ful fol-lower I would be, For by His hand He leadeth me.

Used by per. of BIGLOW & MAIN, owners of Copyright.

40.   LITTLE LAMPLIGHTERS' HYMN.

Selected.   TUNE—"He Leadeth Me."

1 We come, a little infant band,
To light the lamps in heathen land—
To spread the truth that Christ hath
    given,
And win benighted souls to heaven.

Refrain.

We send them light, we send them light,
When earth is wrapped in darkest night;

Though but a little infant band,
We light the lamps in heathen land.

2 "Go preach the gospel," saith the
    Lord;
"Go teach the nations of my Word:
I'll be with you till time shall end—
I can sustain, and I defend."—*Ref.*

43

41. Some Work to Do.

"Lord, what wilt thou have me to do?"

Mrs. Lanta Wilson Smith.   E. C. Phelps.

Allegretto.

1. Give me some work to do, My pre-cious Lord, for Thee, The field is
2. If I may nev-er bear Rich sheaves of gold-en wheat, I still may
3. Show me Thy will, O Lord, What seem-eth to Thee best, I'll glad-ly

large, the reap-ers few, There must be work for me, Work fit-ted for my hand
glean an humble share, To lay at Thy dear feet. And should Thy reapers fail,
do, helped by Thy word, Leaving to Thee, the rest. Thrice hap-py if at last

That holds no spe-cial pow'r: Yet longs to toil at Thy com-mand,
Scorched by the noontide heat; My hands tho' weak, may then a-vail
Be-neath life's set-ting sun, All la-bor o'er, the har-vest past,

Un-til life's lat-est hour. Give me some work to do, Some work to do.
The har-vest to complete. Give me some work to do, Some work to do.
I hear Thy sweet "Well done." Give me some work to do, Some work to do.

42. Who is Ready?

"Go work to-day in my vineyard."—Matt. 21 : 2S.

ANNIE CUMMINGS.   WARREN W. BENTLEY. **By per.**

Spirited.

1. Wait-ing is the gold-en har-vest, Wait-ing is the gold-en grain,
2. Tru - ly is the har-vest plenteous, But the la - bor-ers are few;
3. Will the Mas - ter hold us guiltless If the work be left un-done?
4. Haste, O has-ten, Christian workers : Swift - ly speed the hour a - way;

While the Mas-ter calls for reapers   From the hill-side and the plain.
Pray ye that the Lord of har-vest   Send forth workmen tried and true.
If for lack of la - bor per-ish   Pre-cious souls we might have won?
Hearken to the Mas-ter's warning,   Work ye while 'tis called to - day.

CHORUS.

Who is willing? who is read - y? Who will go and work to - day?

See the gold-en har-vest wait-ing! Who will bear the sheaves a - way?

By permission.
45

43. Gathering Jewels.

Miss P. J. Owens.   Wm. J. Kirkpatrick. By per.

1. Jew - el-gatherers for a crown, Know ye not that many a gem,
2. Souls for whom the Sav-iour died, Souls enwrapp'd in sin - ful night,
3. Gems by cru - el hands de-faced, Pearls in heath-en shad-ows dim,
4. With His blood wash'd white and pure, Graven with His name di-vine,
5. Then our work shall be complete, Then we'll lay our off'rings down,

Now in darkness trampled down, Might be-deck a di - a - dem?
Go and seek them far and wide, They will glit - ter in His sight.
Brill-iants scattered in the waste, We must gath-er up for Him.
These our jew-els shall en-dure, When the stars shall cease to shine.
We will lay them at His feet, He will lift them to His crown.

REFRAIN.

Gathering jewels, precious jew-els, Blood bought souls we seek to bring.

Gathering jew - els, pre-cious jew-els, For the crown of Christ our King.

44. Only a Penny.

Selected.

Mrs. E. B. Hopkins.

DUET.

1. It is on-ly a pen-ny, One bright lit-tle pen-ny, Small
2. Ah! that bright lit-tle pen-ny, That one lit-tle pen-ny, *Great*
3. The dear, lov-ing Sav-iour, Who died on the tree Their
4. 'Twas an an-gel came down And whispered to Ben-ny, This

good it could do, Small good if but any To help the poor heathen Far
good it might do, As have others many, By send-ing the heathen, Far
poor, darken'd souls, From sin to set free; And of a home up in heav-en, That
beau-ti-ful truth Of his bright little penny; So in-to the box For the

o - ver the sea; So I'll go and buy candy, Or, peanuts may-be.
o - ver the sea, The news of the Saviour, Who died on the tree.
beau-ti - ful place, Where God ev - ery tear Shall wipe from the face.
heathen it drops, And the can-dy and peanuts Are left in the shops.

45. Church Rallying Song.

FANNIE J. CROSBY.   JNO. R. SWENEY.

1. Awake! a-wake! the Mas-ter now is call-ing us, A - rise! a - rise! and
2. A cry for light from dy-ing ones in heathen lands: It comes, it comes a-
3. O church of God, ex-tend thy kind, ma-ter-nal arms To save the lost on
4. Look up! look up! the promised day is drawing near, When all shall hail, shall

trusting in His word, Go forth, go forth! proclaim the year of ju - bi-lee, And
cross the ocean's foam; Then haste, oh, haste to spread the words of truth abroad, For-
mountains dark and cold, Reach out thy hand with loving smile to rescue them, And
hail the Saviour King, When peace and joy shall fold their wings in ev'ry clime, And

take the cross, the bless-ed cross, of Christ our Lord.   On,   on, swell the
get - ting not the starv-ing ones at home, dear home.
bring them to the shel - ter of the Saviour's fold.
"Glo-ry, hal - le - lu-jah," o'er the earth shall ring.   On, on, on,

CHORUS.

cho - rus;   On,   on, the morning - star   is shin-ing o'er us;
swell the cho - rus,   On, on, on,

48

On, on, while before us Our mighty, mighty Saviour leads the way:
On, on, on, while before leads the way:

{ Glo-ry, glo - ry, hear the ev-er-last-ing throng }
{ Shout ho-san-na, while we boldly march a-long; } Faithful soldiers here below,

On - ly Je-sus shall we know, Shouting "free salvation" o'er the world we go.

46. A Children's Hymn.

Selected.

Mrs. E. B. HOPKINS.

1. Lit - tle ones in In - dia Lisp the i - dol's praise;
2. Oh! that we could tell them Of a heaven a - bove,
3. Try then, lit - tle chil - dren, Join - ing hand and heart,
4. Lit - tle heath - en chil - dren, By the sums you raise,

Some in homes of dark - ness Pass the wea - ry days.
And that we could teach them Of a Sav-iour's love.
Each to gath - er some-thing, Each to do your part.
Then will hear of Je - sus, And will sing His praise.

49

47. "Precious is the Time."

WM. B. BRADBURY.

GIRLS. — ALL.

1. We must la - bor while 'tis day, Pre-cious is the time;
2. Do we try the right to choose, Pre-cious is the time;
3. Have we sought our fa - ther's love? Pre-cious is the time;
4. We must la - bor while 'tis day, Pre-cious is the time;

GIRLS. — ALL.

Soon the light will fade a - way, Pre - cious is the time;
Not a mo - ment should we lose, Pre - cious is the time;
Live we for our home a - bove? Pre - cious is the time;
Soon the light will fade a - way, Pre - cious is the time;

What - so - e'er we find to do, Let us with our might pur-sue,
Life is like a morn - ing flower, Blooming in a fra-grant bower,
Do we dai-ly kneel in prayer, Thanking God for all His care,
What - so - e'er we find to do, Let us with our might pur-sue,

GIRLS. — ALL.

Keep-ing still one thought in view, Pre-cious is the time.
Drooping, dy - ing in an hour, Pre-cious is the time.
Grate-ful for the gifts we share? Pre-cious is the time.
Keep-ing still one thought in view, Pre-cious is the time.

"Precious is the Time." Concluded.

FULL CHORUS.

Pre-cious is the time, friends! Pre-cious is the time, friends!

We must la - bor while 'tis day, Pre-cious is the time.

48. Hebron. L. M.

ISAAC WATTS, 1719.

1. Je-sus shall reign where'er the sun Does his suc - ces-sive journeys run;
2. To Him shall endless pray'r be made, And endless prais-es crown His head;
3. People and realms of every tongue Dwell on His love with sweetest song,
4. Blessings abound where'er He reigns; The prisoner leaps to lose his chains;
5. Let every crea-ture rise, and bring Pe - cu-liar hon - ors to our King;

His kingdom stretch from shore to shore, Till moons shall wax and wane no more.
His name, like sweet perfume, shall rise With ev-ery morn-ing sac - ri - fice.
And in-fant voices shall proclaim Their ear-ly bless-ings on His name.
The weary find e - ter-nal rest, And all the sons of want are blessed.
An-gels descend with songs again, And earth re-peat the loud A - men.

51

49. Live for Something.

J. H. Tenney.

1. Live for something, be not i - dle, Look a - bout thee for em - ploy;
2. Scat-ter blessings in thy pathway; Gen-tle words and cheering smiles
3. Hearts that are oppress't and wea-ry, Drop the tear of sym-pa - thy,

Sit not down to useless dreaming, La - bor is the sweetest joy.
Bet - ter are, than gold and sil - ver, With their grief dis pell-ing wiles.
Whisper words of hope and comfort Give, and thy re-ward shall be

Folded hands are ev - er wea-ry, Sel - fish hearts are nev-er gay;
As the pleasant sunshine fall-eth Ev - er on the grateful earth,
Joy un - to thy soul re-turn - ing From the sa - cred fountain head,

D. C.—Live for something, etc.

Life for thee hath ma-ny du-ties, Ac - tive be then while you may.
So let sym-pa - thy and kindness, Gladden ev - 'ry darkened hearth.
Freely as thou free-ly giv - eth, Shall the grateful light be shed.

50. **Sunbeams.**

"The King's Messengers."   Mrs. E. B. Hopkins.

1. When the great round sun a - bove us, In the a - ges long gone by,
2. So he marshalled forth an ar - my Of young workers, brave and strong,
3. We are oft-en-times called sunbeams (All un-wor - thy of the name),
4. Yet those lands are wrapped in shadows, Deeper, dark - er than the night;

Glow-ing in his dazzling brightness, First be - gan his course on high,
Sent them on a glorious mis-sion, Bade them la - bor hard and long.
Yet we've learned we have a mis-sion, And to fill it is our aim.
And a cry comes wafted to us, "Send, oh send the gos - pel light!"

His great heart was moved with pit-y, When this vis - ion met his sight,—
And this host of tin - y sunbeams, Thro' the years and years gone by,
We have learn'd of oth - er countries Far a-cross the surging wave,
Will you help us, Christian workers, Blessed so rich - ly with the light,

Worlds on worlds a-bout, be-neath him, Wrapp'd in dense and cheerless night.
Have been fight-ing gloom and darkness, Giv - ing gladness, light, and joy.
Where are mil-lions of dear children Whom our Sav-iour died' to save.
To be shining, cheer-ing sunbeams, For those countries veiled in night?

53

51. Work, for the Night is Coming.

JAMES R. MURRAY.

With Spirit.

1. WORK, for the night is com - ing, PRAY, for the day's at hand;
2. WORK for the souls a - round you, WEEP for your sins, your own;
3. WORK, for the night is com - ing, Prove ev - ery pre-cious hour;

WATCH, for the Mas - ter call - eth, Strive, 'tis your God's com-mand,
FIGHT, for the cross up - on you, WAIT, for the vic - tor's crown,
PRAY, for the day is dawn - ing, Day of the Sav-iour's power.

Now is the time to la - bor, THEN is the judg-ment hour;
WATCH, while you work for oth - ers, PRAY while you wait for power;
REST, when your la - bor's end - ed, Soon shall the glad day come;

Work for the soul's sal - va - tion ev - er, In heaven's e - ter-nal bower.
Watching and wait-ing, al-ways praying, Fill ev - ery gold-en hour.
Day of the bless-ed Saviour's promise, When He shall call us home.

CHORUS.

Work, for the night is com - ing, Pray, for the day's at hand,

54

Work, for the Night is Coming. Concluded.

Watch, for the Mas - ter call - eth, Strive, 'tis your God's com-mand.

52. Father, Lead Thy Little Children.

FANNY J. CROSBY. W. H. DOANE.

1. Fa-ther, lead Thy lit - tle chil-dren Ver - y ear - ly to Thy throne;
2. In the Bi - ble Thou hast taught us All our tho'ts to Thee are known;
3. Tho' the heathen bow to i - dols They have made of wood and stone,
4. Thou dost give us all our com-forts, Ev-ery-thing we call our own

rit.

We will have no gods be-fore Thee; Thou art God, and Thou a - lone.
Thou canst see us in the dark-ness; Thou art God, and Thou a - lone.
We have Christian friends to tell us Thou art God, and Thou a - lone.
Comes from Thee, our Heavenly Fa-ther; Thou art God, and Thou a - lone.

REFRAIN.

Lead, O lead Thy lit - tle chil-dren Ver - y ear - ly to Thy throne;

rit.

We will have no gods be-fore Thee; Thou art God, and Thou a - lone.

53. An Idol.

"Juvenile Miss. Magazine."

1. When grand - pa was a sail - or, he brought an i - dol
2. It's ver - y strange to think a - bout the life that it has
3. Once, when I went to bed a - lone, just to see how 'twould
4. For I think it's very cer - tain, when the hea - then chil - dren

home; It's twice as big as Ma - ry's doll, and
led; I like to play it's liv - ing, and has
feel, I said "Now I lay me" to it, but
knelt, They could - n't learn to love it; and

ug - ly as a gnome; But all my aunts and
think - ers in its head; For then it tells me
some-how 'twas not real; And I felt so fun
prob - a - bly they felt That it was ver - y

56

An Idol. Concluded.

un - cles, pa - pa, and ma - ny
sto - ries, just like sto - ries in a
ny after, that I sold a box of
use - less as an i - dol, but 'twould

more, Have had it for a
book, Of can - ni - bals, and
toys To send a mis - siou-
make An in - ter - est - ing

play - thing when they played up - on the floor.
co - coa-nuts, and conchs, and Cap - tain Cook.
a - ry to the lit - tle hea-then boys.
dol - ly, if 'twas on - ly theirs to take.

57

54. Behold, the Fields are White.

Rev. M. Lowrie Hofford.   Jno. R. Sweney.

1. Look up! be-hold, the fields are white, The har-vest time is near;
2. Look up! be hold, the fields are white, The la - bor-ers are few,
3. Look up! be-hold, the fields are white, The Mas - ter soon will come,

The sum-mons of the Mas-ter falls Up-on the reap-er's ear:
The gath-'ring of the har - vest must By grace de-pend on you:
And car - ry with re-joic - ing heart His gath-ered tro-phies home;

Go forth in - to the gold - en grain And bind the pre-cious sheaves,
Go forth throughout the bus - y world, The world of want and sin,
And can you stand with emp - ty arms, While glad-ly He re - ceives

And gar - ner for the Lord of Hosts The har - vest which He gives.
And gar - ner for the Lord of Hosts Its dy - ing mil - lions in.
From oth - ers in the har - vest field A load of pre - cious sheaves?

Chorus.

Look up! look up! be - hold, the fields are white,
Look up! look up! be - hold! be - hold! the fields are white,

Behold, the Fields are White. Concluded.

The har - vest time is near, The har - vest time is near;
The har - vest time is near, the har - vest time is near:

Look up! look up! be - hold, the fields are white,
Look up! look up!

Look up! be-hold, the fields are white, The har - vest time is near.

55.   Working for Jesus in Youth.

"It is good for a man that he bear the yoke in his youth."—Lam. 3: 27.

JESSE CLEMENT.   A. S. P.

1. Oh, why should we our du - ty shirk, Since well we know it all?
2. Our lit - tle feet, so swift to run In paths with sunshine gay,
3. Our lit - tle lips, so quick to speak The praise of those we love,
4. So shall our days, how-ev - er few, To deeds of love be giv'n;

Our lit - tle hands for Christ should work, Tho' we are young and small.
Why, why should they the path-way shun, Where Je-sus points the way?
Of Him who came our good to seek In praise should joy-ful move.
The way He leads we will pur-sue, And fol-low Him to Heav'n.

By per. of J. W. BISCHOFF.
59

56. Marching On.

"For here have we no continuing city, but we seek one to come."—Heb. 13: 14.

BETH DAY.　　　　　　　　　　　　　　　　J. W. BISCHOFF. By per.

With Spirit.

1. We're a lit-tle band of pilgrims, Marching to the bet-ter land,
2. He who died on Calv'ry's mountain, Is our Captain, kind and true;

To the shin-ing crystal riv-er, Where bright waves wash golden sand;
Come, en-list be-neath His banner; He is wait-ing still for you;

Soon we'll fold our tents in Zi-on, Soon we'll lay our arm-or down,
Marching on-ward to the cit-y Built for us by love di-vine;

Soon we'll bear the palms of victors, Soon we'll wear the star-ry crown.
From the top of faith's high mountain We can see its por-tals shine.

CHORUS.

March on, march on, sing-ing gai-ly, Hal-le-lu-jahs! To our King!

60

King, yes,

Marching On. Concluded.

March on, march on, learning dai - ly, Love and praise a - new to bring.

57. God Speed the Right.

OR, MISSIONARY HYMN.

WILL H. DANA.

1. Far o'er the sea are hea - then lands; No Sav - iour there they know;
2. Their gods are made of wood and stone; These can - not hear them pray;
3. Our hands must work, our hearts must pray, And thus the gos - pel send,

The truth is hid - den from their sight, How long must this be so?
These can - not com - fort in dis - tress, Nor take their sins a - way.
To teach them of the way to Heaven, Of Christ the sin - ner's friend.

CHORUS.

God speed the right, O send them light, Till all who live be-

yond the sea, Shall un - to Je - sus bow the knee.

58. **Migdol. L. M.**

Moderato.

1. Soon may the last glad song a-rise, Thro' all the millions of the skies—
2. Let thrones, and pow'rs, and kingdoms be O-be-dient, migh-ty God, to Thee;
3. O let that glorious anthem swell; Let host to host the triumph tell,

That song of triumph which records That all the earth is now the Lord's.
And over land, and stream, and main, Now wave the sceptre of Thy reign.
Till not one reb-el heart remains, But o-ver all the Sav-iour reigns.

59. **Sicilian Hymn. 8th P. M.**

WILLIAM WILLIAMS, 1772.

1. { O'er the gloomy hills of darkness, Cheer'd by no ce-les-tial ray, }
   { Sun of Righteousness, a-ris-ing, Bring the bright, the glo-rious day: }

Send the gos-pel, Send the gos-pel To the earth's re-mot-est bound.

2 Kingdoms wide that sit in darkness—
Grant them, Lord, the glorious light;
And from eastern shore to western
May the morning chase the night;
And redemption,
Freely purchased, win the day!

3 Fly abroad, thou mighty gospel,
Win and conquer, never cease;
May thy lasting, wide dominion
Multiply and still increase;
Sway thy scepter,
Saviour, all the world around.

60. Hendon. 5th P. M.

Moderato.

1. Has - ten, Lord, the glo-rious time, When be-neath Mes - si - ah's sway,
2. Mightiest kings His power shall own; Hea-then tribes His Name a - dore;

Ev - ery na - tion, ev - ery clime, Shall the gos - pel call o - bey,
Sat - an and his host, o'er-thrown, Bound in chains, shall hurt no more,

Shall the gos - pel call o - bey.
Bound in chains, shall hurt no more.

3 Then shall wars and tumults cease ;
Then be banish'd grief and pain ;
Righteousness, and joy, and peace,
Undisturb'd, shall ever reign.

4 Bless we, then, our gracious Lord ;
Ever bless His glorious Name ;
All His mighty acts record,—
All His wondrous love proclaim:

61. Italian Hymn. 19th P. M.

Allegro.

1. Thou, whose almighty word Chaos and darkness heard And took their flight! Hear us, we
2. Thou, who didst come to bring, On Thy re - deem-ing wing, Healing and sight, Health to the
3. Spir - it of truth and love, Life-giving holy Dove! Speed forth Thy flight; Move o'er the

hum-bly pray, And, where the gospel's day Sheds not its glo-rious ray, "Let there be light!"
sick in mind, Sight to the in-ly blind,—Oh, now to all mankind "Let there be light!"
wa-ter's face, Bear-ing the lamp of grace, And in earth's darkest place, "Let there be light!"

63

62. The Child's Mission.

"Songs for S. Schools and Vestry," 1859. HOYT.

1. Our Je - sus, be - fore He went home To th'house of His kingdom on high,
2. It was not to twelve men a - lone, That th'heavenly commission was given ;
3. If our hearts have been won by His love, We can pray—we can preach—we can sing;

Called all His dis - ci - ples around, And lov-ing - ly bade them good-bye ;
But to all—even children—why not? For of such is the kingdom of heaven.
And, per - haps, to the feet of our Lord, Some younger, some old - er, may bring.

He strengthen'd their eyes to behold The kingdoms that came at His call;
We feel that we've something to do, If not o'er the mountains to roam ;
O, yes, a - bout home is our field ; And Je - sus must mean such as we,

"Go un - to the nations," He said, "And preach my sal-va - tion to all."
And, if we can't RUN thro' the earth, Be sure, we CAN run a - bout home.
When He says, "Go ye, preach the good news, And bring all the peo - ple to me."

63. The Morning Light.

SAMUEL F. SMITH. Tune—WEBB. 7s, 6s.

1. The morn-ing light is break-ing; The dark-ness dis - ap-pears;
2. See hea - then na - tions bend-ing Be-fore the God we love,
3. Blest riv - er of sal - va - tion, Pur-sue thine on - ward way;

The Morning Light. Concluded.

The sons of earth are wak-ing To pen-i-ten-tial tears;
And thousand hearts as-cend-ing In grat-i-tude a-bove;
Flow thou to ev-ery na-tion, Nor in thy rich-ness stay:

Each breeze that sweeps the o-cean Brings tid-ings from a-far,
While sin-ners, now con-fess-ing, The gos-pel call o-bey,
Stay not till all the low-ly Tri-umph-ant reach their home:

Of na-tions in com-mo-tion, Pre-pared for Zi-on's war.
And seek the Sav-iour's bless-ing, A na-tion in a day.
Stay not till all the ho-ly Pro-claim, "The Lord is come!"

64.   THE CHILDREN'S OFFERING.

Selected.

1 The wise may bring their learning,
  The rich may bring their wealth,
And some may bring their greatness,
  And some bring strength and health.
We, too, would bring our treasure
  To offer to the King;
We have no wealth or learning—
  What shall we children bring?

2 We'll bring Him hearts that love Him;
  We'll bring Him thankful praise,
And young souls meekly striving
  To walk in holy ways.
And these shall be the treasures
  We offer to our King;
And these are gifts that even
  The poorest child may bring!

3 We'll bring the little duties
  We have to do each day;
We'll try our best to please him
  At home, at school, at play.
And better are these treasures
  To offer to our King
Than richer gifts without them,
  Yet these a child may bring.

4 Now glory to the Father;
  And glory ever be
To Christ, the loving Saviour,
  Who lived a child like me;
And glory to the Spirit:
  O Three in One, our King,
Accept, 'mid angels' praises,
  The praise a child may bring.

65. Esther. 8s, 7s & 4s.

1. Yes, we trust the day is breaking; Joy - ful times are near at hand;
2. While the foe becomes more daring, While he en - ters like a flood,
3. O, 'tis pleasant, 'tis re - viv - ing To our hearts, to hear, each day,
4. God of Ja - cob, high and glo - rious, Let Thy peo - ple see Thy hand;

God, the mighty God, is speaking, By His word in ev - 'ry land;
God, the Sav-iour, is pre-par-ing Means to spread His truth abroad;
Joy - ful news, from far ar - riv - ing, How the gos-pel wins its way,
Let the gos-pel be vic-to-rious, Thro' the world, in ev-'ry land;

When He choos-es, Dark-ness flies at His com-mand.
Ev - 'ry lan-guage Soon shall tell the love of God.
Those en-lighten-ing Who in death and dark-ness lay.
Then shall i - dols Per - ish, Lord, at Thy com-mand.

66. Zion. 8th P. M.

MRS. CECIL F. ALEXANDER.

1. Souls in hea-then darkness ly - ing, Where no light has broken through;
2. Christians, hearken! none has taught them Of His love so deep and dear;
3. Lo! the hills for har-vest whiten, All a-long each dis-tant shore;

Used by per. of JAMES BAXTER, owner of Copyright.

Zion. Concluded.

Souls that Je-sus bought by dying, Whom His soul in travail knew;—Thousand
Of the precious price that bought them; Of the nail, the thorn, the spear; Ye who
Seaward far the islands brighten, Light of na-tions! lead us o'er: When we

CHORUS.

voic-es Call us, o'er the waters blue. Thousand voices Call us, o'er the waters blue.
know Him,   Ye who know Him, Guide them from their dark-
         Guide them from their darkness drear!   ness drear!
seek them, Let Thy Spirit go before, When we seek them, Let Thy Spirit go before.

67. Little Things.

Moderately Fast.

1. Lit - tle drops of   wa - ter,   Lit - tle   grains of   sand,
2. And the lit - tle   mo - ments,   Hum - ble   though they   be,
3. So our lit - tle   er - rors   Lead the   soul a -   way
4. Lit - tle deeds of   kind - ness,   Lit - tle   words of   love,
5. Lit - tle seeds of   mer - cy,   Sown by   youth-ful   hands,

Make the might - y   o - cean,   And the beau - teous   land.
Make the might - y   a - ges   Of e - ter - ni - ty.
From the paths of   vir - tue   Oft in sin to   stray.
Make our earth an   E - den   Like the heaven a - bove.
Grow to bless the   na - tions,   Far in hea - then   lands.

68. GIVE.

Selected.

1 Only a drop in the bucket,
   But every drop will tell;
The bucket would soon be empty
   Without the drops in the well.

2 Only a poor little penny,—
   It was all I had to give;

But as pennies make the dollars,
   It may help some cause to live.

3 God loveth a cheerful giver,
   Though the gift be poor and small:
What does He think of His children
   When they never give at all?

69. Antioch. C. M.

Isaac Watts. 1709.

1. Joy to the world, the Lord is come! Let earth re-ceive her King;

Let ev'-ry heart pre-pare Him room, And heav'n and nature sing, And
And heav'n and nature

heav'n and na-ture sing, And heav'n, and heav'n and na - ture sing.
sing, And heav'n and nature sing, And heav'n and na - ture sing.

2 Joy to the world, the Saviour reigns!
　Let men their songs employ;
While fields and floods, rocks, hills and
　　plains
　Repeat the sounding joy.

3 No more let sin and sorrow grow,
　Nor thorns infest the ground;

He comes to make His blessings flow,
　Far as the curse is found.

4 He rules the world with truth and
　　grace,
And makes the nations prove
The glories of His righteousness,
　And wonders of His love.

70. Ariel. 4th P. M.

Slowly.

1. Let all on earth their voices raise, To sing the Great Je-ho-vah's praise,
2. He fram'd the globe; He built the sky; He made the shining world on high,
3. Come the great day, the glorious hour, When earth shall feel His saving pow'r.

Ariel. Concluded.

And bless His ho-ly Name: His glory let the heathen know, His wonders to the
And reigns in glory there: His beams are majesty and light: His beauties, how di-
All nations fear His name: Then shall the race of men confess The beauty of His

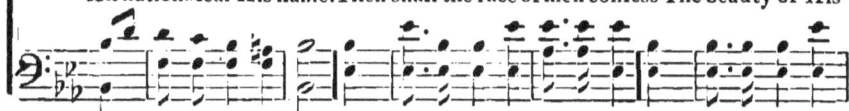

nations show, His sav-ing grace proclaim, His sav-ing grace pro-claim.
vinely bright! His dwelling-place, how fair! His dwelling-place, how fair!
ho - li-ness, His sav-ing grace proclaim, His sav-ing grace pro-claim.

71.   "Jesus Bids Us Shine."

Mrs. Emily Huntington Miller.   Wm. J. Kirkpatrick. By per.

1. Je - sus bids us shine with a pure clear light, Like a lit - tle
2. Je - sus bids us shine first of all for him, Well He sees and
3. Je - sus bids us shine, then, for all a - round Ma - ny kinds of

can - dle burn-ing in the night, In this world of dark - ness
knows it if our lights are dim, He looks down from heav'n to
dark-ness in this world are found; Sin, and want, and sor - row: so

we must shine, You in your lit - tle cor - ner, And I in mine.
see us shine, You in your lit - tle cor - ner, And I in mine.
we may shine, You in your lit - tle cor - ner, And I in mine.

72. A Hymn for Christian Workers.

ANNIE HOWE THOMSON. Chorus by Mrs. E. B. H. WM. B. BRADBURY.

1. O, toil - ers, grow not wea-ry, Wea-ry by the way; Though
2. O, toil - ers, grow not wea-ry, Wea-ry by the way; There're
3. O, toil - ers, grow not wea-ry, Wea-ry by the way; And
4. O, toil - ers, grow not wea-ry, Wea-ry by the way; The

clouds and tem - pests drea - ry May dark - en o'er thy way.
kind - ly words to cheer thee, With faith's un-chang - ing rays;
Sa - tan's hosts shall fear thee, The powers of hell o - bey;
Mas - ter walk - eth near thee, To com - fort and to stay;

The sunshine's still a - bove thee, And soon thou'lt joyful hold The
And foot-prints mark the for - est, And vales and mountains o'er, Of
And on the shores of In - dia, And Chi-na by the sea, The
Thy hands He'll be up-hold - ing, A - mid the fur-rows deep; And

flowers and fruits of har - vest, With sheaves of bur-nished gold.
brave, un-shrink-ing work - ers, Who've has-tened on be - fore.
sow - ing and the REAP - ING Of Christ your Lord shall be.
at life's qui - et even - ing, He'll give thee rest and sleep.

FULL CHORUS.

There's vic - to-ry a-head, yes! vic-to-ry ahead, O'er land and sea sal-

A Hymn for Christian Workers. Concluded.

va-tion's free, For Christ His blood has shed; Yes, Christ His blood has shed; Yes,

Christ His blood has shed; There's vic-to-ry, vic - to - ry, vic - to - ry ahead.

73. Who Should Work for Missions?

"Children's Work for Children." Mrs. E. B. HOPKINS.

1. Who should work for mis-sions, God's king-dom to ad - vance?
2. Why? Be-cause He bids it,—Be - cause so great the need;
3. How long shall we keep at it? How soon may la - bor cease?
4. And so we, here, from year to year Keep up our Mis - sion Band;

Each and all both great and small, Who-ev - er has a chance.
If one wants bread; he *must* be fed, Or he will starve in - deed.
We must keep on till all are won To serve the Prince of Peace.
We must not pause, for still the cause Needs ev - ery heart and hand.

CHORUS.

Why! Because God bids it, Because God bids it, Because He bids us work.

Firm.

1. All hail the power of Je - sus' name! Let an - gels prostrate fall;

Bring forth the roy - al di - a - dem, And crown Him Lord of all.

Bring forth the roy - al di - a - dem, And crown Him Lord of all.

2 Ye chosen seed of Israel's race,
　Ye ransomed from the fall,
Hail Him who saves you by His grace,
　And crown Him Lord of all.

3 Sinners, whose love can ne'er forget
　The wormwood and the gall;
Go, spread your trophies at His feet,
　And crown Him Lord of all.

4 Let every kindred, every tribe,
　On this terrestrial ball,
To Him all majesty ascribe,
　And crown Him Lord of all.

5 O that with yonder sacred throng
　We at His feet may fall;
We'll join the everlasting song,
　And crown Him Lord of all.

75. O FOR A THOUSAND TONGUES TO SING.

TUNE—"Coronation."

1 O for a thousand tongues, to sing
　My great Redeemer's praise;
The glories of my God and King,
　The triumphs of His grace.

2 My gracious Master, and my God,
　Assist me to proclaim,—
To spread, through all the earth abroad,
　The honors of Thy name.

3 Jesus!—the Name that charms our fears,
　That bids our sorrow ceases;

'Tis music in the sinner's ears,
　'Tis life, and health, and peace.

4 He breaks the power of cancell'd sin,
　He sets the pris'ner free;
His blood can make the foulest clean;
　His blood avail'd for me.

5 He speaks,—and list'ning to His voice,
　New life the dead receive;
The mournful, broken hearts rejoice;
　The humble poor believe.

76. Blow the Trumpet.

H. L. GILMOUR. WM. J. KIRKPATRICK. By per.

1. Watchman, blow the gos-pel trum-pet, Ev - 'ry soul a warning give,
2. Sound it loud o'er ev - 'ry hill - top, Gloomy shade and sun-ny plain;
3. Sound it in the hedge and highway, Earth's dark spots where exiles roam,
4. Sound it for the heav-y - la - den, Wea-ry, long-ing to be free;

Who - so - ev - er hears the mes-sage, May re-pent, and turn and live.
O-cean depths re-peat the mes-sage, Full sal - va-tion's glad re-frain.
Let it tell all things are read-y, Fa-ther waits to welcome home.
Sound a Saviour's in - vi - ta - tion, Sweetly say - ing. "Come to me."

CHORUS.

Blow the trumpet, trusty watchman, Blow it loud o'er land and sea; . . .

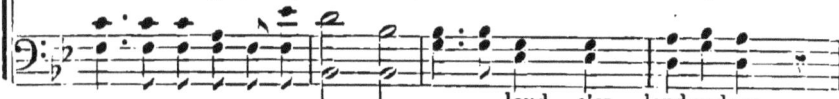

loud o'er land and sea.

God commissions, sound the mes - sage, Ev-'ry cap-tive may be free.

INDEX.